The Po...y
of
Pembrokeshire

The Poetry
of
Pembrokeshire

Edited by Tony Curtis

SEREN BOOKS
*1989

SEREN BOOKS is the book imprint of
Poetry Wales Press Ltd
Andmar House, Tondu Road,
Bridgend, Mid Glamorgan

Selection and Introduction
© Tony Curtis, 1989

ISBN 1-85411-007-1

Cover painting: 'Figure on the Coast Path'
by John Knapp Fisher
Cover design by Jeane Rees

*The publisher acknowledges the financial support of the
Welsh Arts Council*

Typeset in 10½ Plantin by Megaron, Cardiff
Printed by Billing & Sons Ltd., Worcester

CONTENTS

Introduction

The chances are that you are reading this on a visit to Pembrokeshire, or that you are returned from the county and want to remember some aspect of Pembrokeshire. This anthology traces a journey in poetry from the north of the county, around the coast, the haven and the south to finish on the Carmarthenshire border of Dylan Thomas's Sir John's Hill. This book brings together for the first time a comprehensive selection of the finest poems written about a most poetic, beautiful part of Wales. From the anonymous 'praise poem' of the seventh century describing Tenby as "A splendid fort . . . that is stirred by songs", to the poetry of our day which recognises the complex issues of tourism and technological development, it is clear that Pembrokeshire has drawn fine poems from its visiting poets. It has, too, bred poets of its own in its landscape. Giraldus Cambrensis, 'Gerald of Wales', was the first traveller to record in detail impressions of the whole of Wales. As the following extract shows, he had a particular love of Pembrokeshire;

> This is a region rich in wheat, with fish from the sea and plenty of wine for sale. What is more important than all the rest is that, from its nearness to Ireland, heaven's breath smells so wooingly there.
> Of all the different parts of Wales, Dyfed, with its seven cantrefs, is at once the most beautiful and the most productive. Of all Dyfed, the province of Pembroke is the most attractive; and in all Pembroke the spot I have just described is most assuredly without its equal. It follows that in all the broad lands of Wales Manorbier is the most pleasant by far. You will not be surprised to hear me lavish such praise upon it when I tell you that this is where my own family came from, this is where I myself was born.
> — *The Journey Through Wales* translated by L. Thorpe.

Certainly, there is a remarkable number of instances when a writer has been moved to poetry by the landscape and the coastline of Pembrokeshire. The county can boast one of the most notable poets in the Welsh language in Waldo Williams and I am pleased to include his visionary masterpiece 'In Two Fields' as well as poems from the Welsh by T.E. Nicholas and Bobi Jones. These were an omission from a smaller collection which I edited over a decade ago. At that time these fine poems were not readily available in translation. I am happy to include them now and to extend and qualify that earlier selection. In English, too, Pembrokeshire has produced many interesting poets. Roland Mathias and Raymond Garlick, two of the central literary figures in Wales since the war, developed as poets, critics and editors while teaching at Bush Grammar School in Pembroke Dock. Under their editorship a small magazine, *Dock Leaves*, grew into the journal *The Anglo-Welsh Review*. This provided a forum for all the best writing from Wales for over twenty-five years and was dispatched from Pembrokeshire to libraries and readers all over the world. Many of the poets and poems in this book first appeared in those pages.

I moved to Pembrokeshire from Carmarthen in 1960 but I had been coming to the county ever since I could remember. My father was posted here in the war and served on the search-lights at Angle. He met my Lancashire mother who had been sent here as a Land Army girl ('Land Army Photographs' re-creates this time.) Whenever we drove over the old county border near Red Roses on the A48 my father would claim that the weather was brighter, more promising. It was his way of saying that he felt Pembrokeshire to be a place we could escape to. I'm sure that he felt himself to have been displaced by one generation from the county. I have felt that too, ever since those 'story-book childhood weekends' at my Uncle Ivor's in Pwllcrochan, and have tried to capture those feelings of history and belonging in my poem 'Pembrokeshire Seams'. At the turn of the century my grandmother left Jeffreyston to enter the service of a vicar in Carmarthen; her brother left to make his fortune in the coal valleys of Glamorgan, but died a sheep farmer in Canada. Thus a family grows away from its roots. However, the loss of the county's rural workers has been compensated by the steady influx of new settlers drawn to the very seclusion and sense of remoteness which had driven those workers to seek their fortunes elsewhere. But that profound alteration in the society of

Pembrokeshire has caused inevitable problems. "Summer romps in on charabanc and train" (Raymond Garlick) and Milford Haven may "be nothing/ but oil and aftermath" (Peter Preece). *The Poetry of Pembrokeshire* includes several responses to such changes; as John Tripp says in his 'Barafundle' the county presents

> a proud and stubborn line of rock,
> impatient under moon channels
> waiting for the late Atlantic lash,
> turning a storm-eye on frivollers
> but welcoming the rough-weather guest.

John Tripp was one of the most accomplished of Pembroke-shire's 'rough-weather' guests. Every time John visited the county, to perform his poems or simply to feel the "slap of sea wind in my face" ('At Bosherston Ponds'), it seemed that he wrote another poem about his experience of the county. So too, Jean Earle, John Stuart Williams, Jeremy Hooker, Peter Finch, A.G. Prys Jones and others. These writers join with those who were Pembrokeshire born, or who have lived part of their lives in the county to celebrate that which is uniquely the poetry of Pembrokeshire.

Tony Curtis

P.S. An illustration of one of the contentious issues in contemprary Pembrokeshire, that of the two languages, occurred as permissions were sought for the inclusion of poems in this anthology. Such is the concern of R.S. Thomas at the erosion of the Welsh language he declined to have poems included in a book with Pembrokeshire in its title, preferring the Welsh name, Y Bemfro.

DYFED

I speak from deep in Dyfed, little Wales
beyond both Wales and England, where like snails
upon the sea's green leaf the shells and sails

of ships of saints once bustled in the bays,
busy as bees about their lawful ways,
all raising up a honeycomb of praise;

from Dyfed where Pryderi used to ride
and rule the seven green cantrefs; where beside
his bay Giraldus watched the lawn-sleeved tide

fawn on his castle piers at Manorbier,
and sighed, and rode off for another year
to Rome to gain the Holy Father's ear.

I speak from Dyfed, Wales within Wales, world
within world, within whose heart lay curled
the flower from which Four Branches were unfurled —

a green and mighty myth where princes pass
and galleys glide as on a sea of glass,
and poetry the wind that stirs the grass.

Raymond Garlick

LANDSCAPE IN DYFED

Because the sea grasped cleanly here, and there
Coaxed too unsurely until clenched strata
Resisted, an indecision of lanes resolves
This land into gestures of beckoning
Towards what is here and beyond, and both at hand.

Walk where you will, below is an estuary.
In advance to a fleeting brightness you traverse
So many shoals of the dead who have drowned
In stone, so many hibernations
Of souls, you could be in phantom country.

But the tapers of gorse burn slowly, otherwise.
And here are rock cathedrals which can be
As small as your span. And, at the water's edge,
A struck havoc of trees clutches the interim season,
The given roots bare, seeming to feed on the wind;

And in their limbs what compass of sun
Is contained, what sealed apparitions of summer,
What transfixed ambulations. If you could cut
Right to the heart and uncouple the innermost rings
Beyond those nerves you would see the structure of air.

John Ormond

PRESELI

Wall of my boyhood, Foel Drigarn, Carn Gyfrwy, Tal Mynydd,
Backing me in all independence of judgment,
And my floor from Y Witwg to Wern and down to Yr Efail
Where the sparks spurted that are older than iron.

And in the yards, on the hearths of my people —
Breed of wind, rain, and mist, of sword-flag and heather,
Wrestling with the earth and the sky and winning
And handing on the sun to their children, from their stooping.

Memory and symbol, a reaping party on their neighbour's
        hillside,
Four swaths of oats falling at every stroke,
And a single swift course, and while stretching their backs
Giant laughter to the clouds, a single peal of four voices.

My Wales, land of brotherhood, my cry, my creed,
Only balm for the world, its message, its challenge,
Pearl of the infinite hour, pledge given by time,
Hope of the long journey on the short winding way.

This was my window, the harvesting and the shearing.
I beheld order in my palace there.
A roar, a ravening, is roaming the windowless forest.
Let us guard the wall from the beast, keep the well-spring free
        of the filth.

Waldo Williams

(Translated by Joseph P. Clancy)

WILD ORCHIDS

Hot stink of orchid in the woods at Fforest.
Downstream of the waterfall I breathed
their scent and touched their purple towers,
the swollen root that cures the King's Evil
and makes the heart hot. Not flowers to share
to bring home for a jar.
Ophelia's long purples, tragic flowers.
You could believe they grew beneath the cross
and no amount of rain could wash the blood
from their stained leaves.

They called and called but I would not hear,
mixing their voices with waves and water.
Crouched in the blackthorn tunnel the cattle made
as they swayed their way to the sea, loosed
from the beudy by Gwilym and slapped free,
I was hooked on dens and secret places,
illicit books, visions and diaries
and the tomcat scent of orchids. Nothing
would fetch me out but hunger, or the sound
of shadows stepping closer.

Gillian Clarke

from ST DAVID'S HEAD

Salt sprays deluge it, wild waves buffet it, hurricanes rave;
Summer and winter, the depths of the ocean girdle it round;
In leaden dawns, in golden noon-tides, in silvery moonlight
Never it ceases to hear the old sea's mystical sound.
Surges vex it evermore
By gray cave and sounding shore.

Think of the numberless far-away centuries, long before man,
When the hot earth with monsters teemed, and with
monsters the deep,
And the red sun loomed faint, and the moon was caught fast in
the motionless air,
And the warm waves seethed through the haze in a secular
sleep.
Rock was here and headland then,
Ere the little lives of men.

Over it long the mastodons crashed through the tropical
forest,
And the great bats swooped overhead through the half-
defined blue;
Then they passed, and the hideous ape-man, speechless and
half-erect,
Through weary ages of time tore and gibbered and slew.
Grayer skies and chiller air,
But the self-same rock was there.

So shall it be when the tide of our greatness has ebbed to the
shallows;
So when there floats not a ship on this storm-tossed
westerly main,
Hard by, the minster crumbles, the city has shrunk to a
village;
Thus shall we shrink one day, and our forests be pathless
again;

And the headland stern shall stand,
Guarding an undiscovered land.

Sir Lewis Morris

ST DAVID'S CATHEDRAL

Austerely beautiful it stands
In this green-bastioned glen,
The jewel of the fabled Western land
Beyond the haunts of men;
For here the Norman Leia dreamed and planned,
Building this massive nave,
Pier, arch and architrave,
With skilled, unerring hand,
Of purple stone that knew the shock and roar
Of thundering seas upon the fortressed shore;
And here the Western Wykeham, Gower, wrought
With sure, consumate art,
His chambered rood-screen, where, enmeshed and caught,
In sparkling cusp and crocket here
About his princely bier
And all the visions of a poet's heart.
And like an Oriental dream,
Above the high, triumphant nave is spread
Pole's rich, grey roof of fretted arch and beam,
Each gorgeous carven pendant overhead,
Like damask out of Araby,
While round about the thrusting lantern tower
Burn colour and red heraldry.

Without, stands Gower's palace in array
Of lordly halls and ageless, proud arcades,
Built in the soaring splendour of his prime,
Transfigured by the crafty hands of time
To mellow richness of sublime decay.

So from this place of beauty never fades
The glory of the builders, those who made
With pious, artist hands and hearts aglow
This jewel of the fabled Western land,
In memory, long years ago,

Of one who lived and prayed
In this green-bastioned glen,
St David, Cymric Prince of Christian men.

A.G. Prys-Jones

AT THE SEA'S EDGE, IN PEMBROKESHIRE

Peter de Leia, dead eight
hundred years, began this
structure. Not having the
saint's art, nor learned
his psalter from a gold-
beaked pigeon, he built
in common stone. He exalted
labour into a stone praise.

Nor was he baptised in live
waters conveniently burst
forth to supply the shaken
drops for that ceremony. To
reach his pulpit he climbed
a joiner's steps, did not expect
the ground to lift in a sudden
hillock so that he could preach
in open piety to the rapt Welsh.

When he laid down the square-
ended presbytery, with aisles,
transepts, tower and nave, he saw
his masons bleed if the chisel
slipped. One fell in his sight
from the brittle scaffolding
and the two legs snapped
audibly, hitting the ground.
He had not the saint's skill

to stop that falling which must
fall. Such clear faith was not
possible, the rule of the world
grown strong. He knew that right
building was a moral force, that
stone can grow. An earthquake

has tested this cathedral. In
Pembrokeshire, near the saint's
river, at the edge of the sea,

de Leia built well, saw stone
vault and flower. A plain man,
building in faith where God
had touched the saint, he saw
the miracle which is not swift
visitation, nor an incredible
suspension of the commonplace,
but the church grown great about us,
as if the first stone were a seed.

Leslie Norris

CROMLECH PENTRE IFAN

Just here, at dusk,
the light may move
so many, varied ways
that huddled, staring,
by the capstones' lintel buttress
we shudder in the silence.
The still, oppressive presence
of the place serves now
to bend the mind,
transcend long years
to when the dark men
phantomed through the cromlech's
legs of stone.
Their eyes black charcoal
with the fervour of the dance,
some pagan incantation
to their gods still ringing,
pulsing centuries of pain.

No flight of fantasy —
the dark ones still remain,
their white, blanched bones
still churning with the richness
of the soil; sleeping gods
still watching in the night fire's
ravenous glow.

Like some prehistoric phoenix
their ashes move, grow solid
as flint-edged eyes
conspire.

Phil Carradice

RAMSEY ISLAND

Drab gorse crouches;
and the stunted thorn, its back bent
from the lash, fleeing
the wind —
but root-bound,
like the girl becoming laurel.

There are no nymphs or gods pursuant
here;
barely a crippled tree is bared
against the sky.

Only wind, running
the turf one way like a close pelt;
and precipices to the sea.

Even men, who root anywhere,
landed, lasted a few brute seasons out,
were gone.
There is nothing to grip on.

*

The island's a bird sanctuary now.
Like the leaning wind, it has
prevailed,
becoming finally what it always was.

The once-gutted stone
habitation has been renovated for the warden.
With his deep-freeze, radio and books,
his sinecure's
as steady as a lighthouse job.
He'll last here longer than those
who had to, and couldn't —
each crude, repetitive meal

earned
singly, eaten
after darkness off the day's bare plate —

the fish-taste of gull-eggs;
a rim of chipped bone.

*

Cut off in winter
for weeks at a stretch, you hunched to stare across
the straits and see
a man ploughing a field dark
on the mainland in a cloud of gulls,
as if on the next hill.

Here the dirt was
thinner than the scalp on your skull.

But there were worse straits —
the rock was
fast;
you thought of those out in that running sea.

A fine day
was not a respite but increase of labour.

Yet there were the moments: going
out at morning;
the sea sometimes, when the back straightened.

In a bleak, intermittent
diary, kept a full year he survived
on the island, Ivor Arnold, poor
at spelling, and grudging
his entries

like flour or paraffin or twine,
recorded of a day in March, 1908:

'Wind S. A fine day. I could hear
Will Morris Pencarnan talking
to his horses yesterday from Congrwn Bach.'

Duncan Bush

IN TWO FIELDS

Where did the sea of light roll from
Onto Flower Meadow Field and Flower Field?
After I'd searched for long in the dark land,
The one that was always, whence did he come?
Who, oh who was the marksman, the sudden enlightener?
The roller of the sea was the field's living hunter.
From above bright-billed whistlers, prudent scurry of lapwings,
The great quiet he brought me.

Excitement he gave me, where only
The sun's thought stirred to lyrics of warmth,
Crackle of gorse that was ripe on escarpments,
Hosting of rushes in their dream of blue sky.
When the imagination wakens, who calls
Rise up and walk, dance, look at the world?
Who is it hiding in the midst of the words
That were there on Flower Meadow Field and Flower Field?

And when the big clouds, the fugitive pilgrims,
Were red with the sunset of stormy November,
Down where the ashtrees and maples divided the fields,
The song of the wind was deep like deep silence.
Who, in the midst of the pomp, the super-abundance,
Stands there inviting, containing it all?
Each witness' witness, each memory's memory, life of each life,
Quiet calmer of the troubled self.

Till at last the whole world came into the stillness
And on the two fields his people walked,
And through, and between, and about them, goodwill widened
And rose out of hiding, to make them all one,
As when the few of us forayed with pitch forks,
Or from heavy meadows lugging thatching of rush,
How close we came then, one to another —
The quiet huntsman so cast his net round us!

Ages of the blood on the grass and the light of grief,
Who whistled through them? Who heard but the heart?
The cheater of pride, and every trail's tracker,
Escaper from the armies, hey, there's his whistling —
Knowledge of us, knowledge, till at last we do know him!
Great was the leaping of hearts, after their ice age.
The fountains burst up towards heaven, till,
Falling back, their tears were like leaves of a tree.

Day broods on all this beneath sun and cloud,
And Night through the cells of her wide-branching brain —
How quiet they are, and she breathing freely
Over Flower Meadow Field and Flower Field —
Keeps a grip on their object, the fields full of folk.
Surely these things must come. What hour will it be
That the outlaw comes, the hunter, the claimant to the breach.
That the Exiled King cometh, and the rushes part in his way?

Waldo Williams

(Translated by Tony Conran)

ON WEUN CAS' MAEL

I walk once more on Weun Cas' Mael
As its gorse bushes, that never fail,
Declare that winter, withered and frail,
    Is losing the day.
'The blue of our bountiful sky will prevail,'
    Their faith's flames say.

And today at moments, clear and still,
Above the earth that's sodden, chill,
The skylark gives a lengthy trill,
    Bright song unchained,
True inspiration's trust and thrill,
    Hope of the land.

O! blossoms on the roughest plant,
O! song upon the steep ascent —
The same sweetness, from the same strength,
    The dear delight
Of the bare acres that hide their worth
    From worldly sight.

O! Wales of the cairn and the dark moorland,
Nursery of independence of judgment,
Above the rubble your strength will stand
    From age to age.
Draw us to you: make us a part
    Of your life and ways.

In your grand austerity
You wakened men to charity,
Harmonious their society —
    Backed by your strength,
Their benign order flourished freely,
    With none a slave.

Bring us back. From the bonds of steel
Deep throbs of pain cross Weun Cas' Mael:
In Tre Cŵn's underground men kneel
    To the false power.
Raise us from our caves to the hill
    Whose winds are pure.

As to the skylark in his gyre
Give from your soil the aim and fire,
Teach us for your sake to nurture
    Each gift in bud.
And through your strength, for your honour
    Make me your bard.

Waldo Williams

(Translated by Joseph P. Clancy)

TO A SPARROW

(Swansea Prison 1940)

Look, here's another bread-crumb for your piping,
And a piece of apple as a sweetener.
It gladdens me to hear your steady pecking;
It's good to see your cloak of grey once more.
You've travelled here, perhaps, from Pembroke's reaches,
From the gorse and heather on Y Frenni's height,
And maybe on grey wing you've trilled your measures
Above fair Ceredigion at dawn's first light.
Accept the bread: had I a drop of wine
Pressed from a distant country's sweet grape-cluster,
We two could take, amid war's turbulence,
Communion, though the cell lacks cross and altar.
The bread's as holy as it needs to be,
Offering of a heart not under lock and key.

T.E. Nicholas

(Translated by Joseph P. Clancy)

DEFENCE OF THE WEST

HMS *Felicity in Fishguard*

'We have the most
sophisticated gear,' the captain said.
'Can I see it?'
'No.'
'Why not?'
'It's secret.'
'What do you aim at?'
'Towed targets.'

She sat in the bay
a frigate of deadly silence
that could blow old Fishguard
into the water. The captain's
voice was royal yacht squadron,
his intelligence as crisp as his white
shirt; in blue cummerbund and black
dancing pumps, he gave me
pink gin in the teak wardroom
and produced his handsome young officers
who were ready for World War III.
('We could put up a pretty good show,'
a rosy-cheeked buy said to me).

Layers of steel hid technology
that could pinpoint a raft,
knock out a port miles away.
We chugged back to the quay in a launch,
and by dawn Felicity had gone
to shoot missiles at floating planks.

John Tripp

SLEEPING OUT ON PEN CAER

We are not mystics
Though this was their country:
Crested headlands
Like stone dragons drinking.

Haunt of hermit and guillemot;
Swirl of white islands
Where the current bore them.
Crucifix for pilot, among the seals.

We could have had a warm bed,
But chose discomfort, cold,
Feeling the earth
With our bones, under
The immense pale drifts of the Milky Way.

We have our whisky and tobacco.
We belong as much to jets
That pass above, as to the stars.

Before light the gulls' cries
Wake an older earth; hoarse and shrill.
The salt cry of rocky islands.

The sun appears, a red ball
Over the volcanic crags
Of Garn Fawr.

Out at sea the esses of a breeze
Lie like the marks of a lash
Flicked on a smooth insensible hide.

Jeremy Hooker

SKOKHOLM

At dusk great rafts of shearwaters
Rise and fall with the slow tide
And the island's edge and colour
Lose definition. The wide
Fingered buzzard spirals down.
No wind sucks the sun-dried
Grass: the air contracts, still, but alive . . .

Suddenly the mist explodes, the sense
Is bruised by buffeting wings, the night
Is luminous with noise as bird after bird
Comes swinging home. I light
My torch, and catch one spread on the turf
Before its gull-proof hole. It hooks its wings
And slides below, leaving flecks of surf
To trace its track on the yellow grass.

In the iridescent morning air
Below the singing bird-shot sky.
Their sharp wings spread like arms,
The lost shearwaters lie
Eviscerated by the gulls.
Those without deep-shelters die.

John Stuart Williams

SEAL

When the milk-arrow stabs she comes
water-fluent down the long green miles.
Her milk leaks into the sea, blue
blossoming in an opal.

The pup lies patient in his cot of stone.
They meet with cries, caress as people do.
She lies down for his suckling, lifts him
with a flipper from the sea's reach
when the tide fills his throat with salt.

This is the fourteenth day. In two days
no bitch-head will break the brilliance
listening for baby-cries.
Down in the thunder of that other country
the bulls are calling, and her uterus is empty.

Along and hungering in his fallen shawl
he'll muzzle the Atlantic and be gone.
If that day's still his moult will lie
a gleaming ring on sand
like the noose she slips on the sea.

Gillian Clarke

GANNET

hangs on the wind on motionless wings
and falls a hundred feet

on a gleam of fish.
The sea gasps

as the hiss of iron
in the farrier's bucket.

The black wave,
a white-hot knife of light,

sea's retina dazzled
by the sign of the cross.

Gillian Clarke

EXPEDITION SKOMER

A boast of boys and a giggle of girls
in a boat off the higgledy piggledy coast
that wriggles through caves and coves and curls

to the waves of the holy bay of Saint Bride;
a boat that, perverse of nature, behaves
like a sliding, unstrapped saddle astride

to bottle-green, battle-bright hogsback sea.
So we rear our rocking-horse way across
from the wracks of Wales to the black bohea

of the bay of Skomer, the sea-green dome
of the pirate island with the cruel Norse name
where seals and smugglers have felt at home,

and Look! (shout the children) A puffin — there!
as we shrug round another shoulder of stone
and the sound of the outboard stutter and swear

as our heel splutters out, and the silken sand —
saffron and smooth — slides under the keel.
Then, praising God, I land.

Raymond Garlick

SOLVA HARBOUR

Always one hill brilliant and one dark,
In memory — sharing the long curve
To sunset. Seas leap and fall
With a white sigh around two rocks,
Markers and exclaimers
Under whatever sky,
As we are ourselves

When we return, to breathe upon
Fading light. Is such remembering
A life form? Will it revive
Peripheral presences?
Floaters in the iris,
Vague to a central vision
Dazzled with happiness. . . .

Forms we would now acknowledge, name
As witnesses: whether or not aware
On that day, how we sat stunned
In our own silence, like the boats
In the emptied harbour,
Waiting for inflowing tide
To move them again.

There was a girl running to swim
In the evening: she would be old now.
We scarcely noticed her pass
But the years insist, she was beautiful.
We would recreate her
Out of the mindless joy
Through which we sensed her. . . .

She: and the flowers in our colours,
The seabirds. All we did not heed
Being on that day our own

Adamant life. In a sunned mirror,
Brighter than experienced. . . .
Though it blows up for storm
And the harbour's grey.

Jean Earle

BOY IN A BOAT

In Solva harbour the sea makes its peace
waiting half-asleep for the turning tide.
The haltered boats, white in faceless sun,
ride its slow certainty, while out in the stream
a small boy fishes away time,
safe from the cold drag, the weight
of unseen fathoms shrouding the shifting dead.
His spinning hook cuts the green light
and his line strains towards the far farers,
silent sharers of his waiting tide.

John Stuart Williams

OUT AT THE EDGE

(Pembrokeshire Coast Path in Winter)

The wind comes in off the sea at Nolton
filling the Mariner's car park with sand.
There are no cars.
At the tide edge a lone tripper
throws pebbles through the drizzle.
I watch, dripping, with two ducks
and a chicken,
from the bottom of a barren hedge.
When I climb the track
towards Druidstone I leave bootmarks
like fossils in the fluid mud.
Why do it?
Beauty, light, passion.
Who knows?
I get the feeling that if there is
an edge to this world then it is here.
From the headland I stare out at America
but don't see it.
Mist, distance, earth's curvature,
or maybe it just isn't there.

Peter Finch

TRAVELLING

Leaving Croesgoch, the night closes in
locking the land firm
as we drive southward home.

Past Solva, and the tight twists
of the road spiral us towards sea.

Newgate strung by phosphorescent surf,
windsong and the slush of pebbles:
rain rinsing through our headlights' mist.

Six months from this Boxing Day
and our limousine inching
away from clustered scrapers,
down the cloudbursted freeway
over the Hudson to Kennedy:
a grounded flight,
the banal limbo of a terminal wait.

Hung like waves between two points,
all our time we are travelling,
unwinding the road home,
the wipers an insistent metronome,

eyes cutting into the night
needing water and light
water and light.

Tony Curtis

MILFORD HAVEN

If it were not for
the bent wind
and the spinning sea
or the red earth
and the flower fight,
there would be nothing
but oil and aftermath.

There would be nothing
but pipes and tubing,
strewn intestines,
functioning, obscene;
belly tanks
and flame belch,
moving and motoring blood.

The spirit of life
is dirt,
scum on the boat bow,
black on the wave tip,
and the heart is full
of money,
beating
and paid to be full.

But there is the bent wind
and the sea spinning
even though the earth
is redder than before.

Peter Preece

THE FISHING LASS OF HAKIN

Ye sailors bold both great and small
That navigate the ocean,
Who love a lass that's fair and tall,
Come hearken to my motion;
You must have heard of Milford Haven,
All harbours it surpasses,
I know no port this side of heaven
So famed for handsome lasses.

In Milford on your larboard hand
We found a town called Hakin,
The snuggest place in all the land
For lads inclined to raking;
There all the girls were cleanly dressed,
As witty as they are pretty,
But one exceeded all the rest,
And this was charming Betty.

A fisherman her father was,
Her mother a fishwoman,
And she herself a fishing lass
Perhaps possessed by no man;
She'd bait her hook with lug or crab,
No fisherman so nimble,
And at her oar she was a dab,
But never at her thimble.

Assist me, all the watery tribe,
I find my wit a-flagging
As I endeavour to describe
This precious pearl of Hakin;
Ye mermaids tune my merry song,
And Neptune bless my darling,
Your smoking altars shall ere long
Be spread with sole and sparling.

Her fishing dress was clean and neat,
It set me all a-quaking,
I loved her and could almost eat
This maiden ray of Hakin;
If ere you saw a cuttle fish,
Her breasts are more inviting,
Like shaking blubbers in a dish,
And tender as a whiting.

Her cheeks are as a mackerel plump,
No mouth of mullet moister,
Her lips of tench would make you jump,
They open like an oyster;
Her chin as smooth as river trout,
Her hair as rockfish yellow,
God's Sounds! I view her round about
But never saw her fellow.

When hungry people write for bread,
Whom they call poetasters,
They talk of fires in topmast head,
Of Pollax and of Castor's;
Her eyes afford a brighter mark
Than all those flashy meteors,
Like Milford Lights even in the dark
Revealing all her features.

Whene'er a smile sits on her lip
I'm brisk as bottled cider,
I quite renounce and leave my ship
And never can abide her;
Whene'er she speaks, so sweet her tone
I leap like spawning salmon,
And when she sings I'm all her own,
I serve no Jove nor Mammon.

But if she frowns I'm gone to pot,
As dead as pickled herring,
The muscles of my heart must rot
And split from clew to earring;
Then in my hammock sink me deep
Within the sight of Hakin,
Then sure she'll melancholy weep
As turtles at their taking.

Let doctors kill, let merchants cheat,
Let courtiers cog and flatter,
Let gluttons feed on costly meat,
Let me have Betty's platter;
To mess with her I'd spend my days
On pilchard and on poor-John,
Let richer folks have if they please
Their turbot and their sturgeon.

Sir Lewis Morris

AFON CLEDDAU

(at Llawhaden)

With no witness in my ears but the evening, I entered her
   presence
And held my spirit upon her, close to her spirit.
I fed my soul by looking at her fluent moving.

In approaching through Bethesda, I had not been ready
   To take anything from her arrival. Wasn't everything
Important but this? And then for a moment, while I was

Descending, here on the edge of the bank, half a yard
   From the water, my whole mind fell silent.
Everything scattered like hay: I lost my grip on every sort

Of credo and of facts. And with my life-force a wasteland
   I saw her — all the joy of her, her bent
For laughing, her way of living, with her frivolous
     wholesome

Bubbling. She has an arm round the dark meadows' collar
   That holds the hillside and the castle: a nation's sinew
That also stretches straight beneath my falling.

She is always there, her foot pretty in nettles;
   Her stars run whitely like a little lad; from the air
The praise of gnats swarms down to fly through her breath.

Oh! her slow brightness that drowns the moon is
     disinfecting,
   And her heart is wild beneath the hills. She offers
Her shapeliness to the evening, though so cold its
     misunderstanding.

I stretch arm to river, good medicine of tranquillity,
And draw it into my dull veins before venturing back to the
plague.

Bobi Jones

(Translated by Joseph P. Clancy)

LANDSKER

So this is it. The Landsker Line
That has lasted almost a thousand years;
The line that splits us into two —
Keeping the savage Welshman out,
They told me in school. Our solid castles,
Limestone built, secured the rich lands
Of the south against the foxy,
Wily men from those blue, distant hills
With their peasant language that outraged
Our cultured ears. Our Saxon tongue
Disguised the names they left behind
As was our right. Even our churches,
Towered to warn of any approach,
Took on their saints for us to own.
It all made sense. We did not want
The heathered slopes and rocky bays
Where they still lived. Rightly ours
The rich, level, loamy soil
We took from them by sword and guile.
In time our castles tumbled down.
But still we ruled. Though we were few,
We turned the southern Pembroke men
Against their kin above the line.
We even gulled them into wars
By waving their flag for our king.
And they let go their simple lives
From both sides of Landsker's spell
When we told them they were us,
And gave their charismatic leaders
Bright rewards, echoing names,
Pieces of land to buy them off —
Their own land to buy their minds.
Their leaders' lies are legendary:
They still go on. And this is it.
The Landsker Line. Somewhere, between

These neighbour farms it still exists
Simply and efficiently,
Sharper than any blackthorn hedge,
Higher than any dyke or wall,
Wider than any stretch of sea,
Because it is invisible,
Because we told them it was there.
And they still shout our message on.

Of course we know the danger is
That one dark, winter day
Someone will betray the cause,
Telling them the grinning truth —
Like the boy who told the naked king
And made the wakened people laugh.
But by then we shall have moved
Up into those holy hills
That were always a threat on clear mornings
Before the rain, their sudden looming
Striking their own echoed cries
As they seemed to lunge south.
But if they ever cross this line
Arms outstretched to re-unite,
They will meet us everywhere,
Living in their rebuilt farms,
Around the lobsterpotted bays.

So let me repeat, as I walk this line:
This is Landsker. Somewhere it is here.

Cliff James

PWLLCROCHAN

I spent weeks down here:
Spring and Autumn planting and picking,
thick wedges of bread and tea,
hands smelling of earth and potato juice;
story-book childhood weekends of stolen
apples, blown birds' eggs, trespassing;
rainy evenings exploring the smugglers' cellar,
shadows jerked alive by the throbbing light generator.

The Old Rectory has gone —
scraped flat for a Texaco car-park,
abandoned after six months.
Now, outbuildings enclose a grassy space,
an ache of absence.
We walk the rutted lake to the bay:
from the narrow, stone bridge inland
the refinery spreads its shining tentacles,
its waste-burner roaring, glowing through the day.

The small bay is thick with reeds, wiry grass:
stream trickling over wellington-hungry mud
to slide beneath shells and sandstone shale
into the once-secret Haven.
Across the deep water from our fishing rocks
the gantries suckle from fat tankers,
steel arteries pulse away through the hills.

Looking back up to the road
I frame you in the camera lens,
centred by the cleft of the sloping fields.
You turn, Gareth smiles in your arms
and the photo worked perfectly,
bringing you into focus
and leaving all the rest behind.

As we walk back to the car, stepping from
bank to tussock, the marks of our weight in the mud stay,
draw an ooze of oil to rainbow our way.

Tony Curtis

JACK WATTS

squints across a sprouting field,
chews at a leaf, then weighs your crop
to the nearest bag.

Soft cap down to the eyes
and what had been somebody's suit
held by baling cord;
he is pigmented with dirt
as if washing would have drained
away the year's knowledge.

The whole county waits:
in April the Pembrokeshire Earlies come
a stiff, dark green out of the ground.
Jack and his tribe pour
like Winter rats from their cottage.

Jack stops at the stile,
pushes the cap back to the perch of his head,
then walks along a row to what becomes
the centre of the field.
He delivers a potato from the earth,
soil spilling from the web of tubers,
shaking from the clumps.
He scrapes through dirt and skin;
the sweet flesh goes between his leather lips,
a nugget lodging in the jags of his teeth.

He closes his eyes on the taste —
it is the soil crumbling, the crush
of frost, the rain carried in on the sea,
the sweat of planting.

He holds the ridged sweetness to his nose,
between finger and thumb it glistens,
the rarest egg, the first
potato and the last.

Tony Curtis

LAND ARMY PHOTOGRAPHS

How lumpy and warlike you all looked,
leaning against the back of a truck,
hair permed underneath headscarves;
in make-up, corduroys, with long woollen socks
— the uniform completed by a khaki shirt and tie.

You are posed in a harvest field:
long wooden rakes and open necks in one
of those hot wartime summers. Fifteen of you
squinting into the camera,
and the weaselly Welsh farmer, arms folded,
his cap set at an angle
that would be jaunty for anyone else.
He's sitting there in the middle, not really
knowing about Hitler, or wanting to know,
but glad to have all those girls
with their English accents and their laughs.

Mother, how young you look, hair back, dungarees,
a man's head at your shoulder.
You girls cleared scrub-land, burned gorse,
eyes weeping as the smoke blew back;
milked cows and watched pigs slaughtered.
You, who could not drive,
drove tractors with spiked metal wheels, trucks.
And once, on the Tenby to Pembroke road,
along the Ridgeway, they had you working flax.
For two days only it bloomed,
the most delicate blue flowers.
Like wading into a field of water.

I see you piling the gorse. Dried spikes
flaring into silver ferns, and smoke
twisting from the piles as the wind comes in

gusts, cool from the sea, the gulls drifting
lazily on the flow.

                    And then,
one of them, too steady, too level, becoming
a Sunderland coasting in to Milford Haven:
over Skomer, Skokholm, Rat Island, over the deep water;
and, though you do not know it, over a man
who is smoking, scraping field potatoes
for the searchlight crew's supper,
who pulls and unpeels the rabbit they have trapped,
joints and throws it into the steaming stew,
the oil-drum perched over an open fire;
the man who looks up, the man who is my father,
watching the white belly of that flying boat
cut into the Haven.

                                        Tony Curtis

THE WEATHER VANE

The wind is rising:
the plastic man turns his handle
and the paddles go over and over.
A trick of the eye.
The paddles turn the man,
the wind animates him.

An evening in September: light
blue and brown streaking the West sky.
The vane's tail-fin catches and spins
the whole thing on its pivot.
So the man bends and works, spins
to hold in the trough of the wind.
Dad, it was you painted the post
and fixed it firm. Last year.
That same wind moves your ashes tonight in the sea
and the grass in Pembrokeshire.

In the summer I saw the whole stretch of our coast
from thirty five thousand feet.
Flat Holm to Pennar and not a cloud.
South Wales spread out like a school atlas,
so green and small before the hours of ocean.
It was like looking back on our lives.

The last light's fallen away.
There's no man or paddles or wishing well.
You and I separated now by a long year,
going our ways into the second winter.

Tony Curtis

FRESHWATER WEST

Over, break white and wash swiftly
Around this rock where earlier
Suds sand hiding swish and uncover.
Press, press on the slope of glass
Sliding over, over. White and pass
Me, wish peace and deliver
From hope, all you byegones, hush
And recover. Break ground and foam
Over and over, newcomers, beat
And surround, beat and surround
And repeat ad finitum, everyone
Beat till the few and the best of these summers
Of mine are as sand, over
And many and meaningless, far beyond
Hand and all measure, lost whereunder
Danger and no man's cast discover.

Wish. I am hidden already. Have I
A wish? Only for peace in the sudden
Hillock of glass and the green
Lease of the tide. Pass,
Pass on your way, over and over,
Beat and digress and repeat, young
Diver and mass old-white
With frays, press and retreat and recover:
Of your half wish there is nothing lost,
Nothing of praise and success, over
And over spoken, nothing but gland
And flesh, a rushing atomiser
Broken like sand from off the human coast.

Roland Mathias

FRESHWATER WEST REVISITED

After six years this winter has not changed,
Encounter of sea and land, ellipses
Of force that intersect and flow boldly
Into and round each other as though
The air were party to either, *socius*
Only because savage both determine so.

This is no place of secondary forms,
Pretty distractions, heights of cliffs
Or trees, not far-out ships puffing
Irrelevantly of other shores and clashes.
Here the brute combers build the waterhead
And grass girds up the dunes the shock washes.

Away inland one can forget so much,
Ease the elliptical abrasions, bandage, duck,
Sidestep the bull-nosed rushes of a wrong
On right, proffer a parody to the back of it.
This cold October morning lays the action bare:
Sea is, and land, and bloodwreck where they meet.

Roland Mathias

AT BOSHERSTON PONDS

In November it is desolate, and distant
from the ruck of summer. The mashed carpet of leaves
lie apple-rust in the gravegaps,
their season done. Waves of high grass
wash about the church, drowning
the sunk mounds, the lopsided slabs
askew from weather and dying stock.
Names illegible beneath layered moss
clip me to futility, yet give that mild
pleasure we feel in cemeteries.
I am cousined to them by nothing
but a moment in Wales
and the loom of skulled union
under roof of turf with the winning maggot.
History on this dot of the map
is sufficient to make me limp
a foot high. In my pocket a poem
shrivels to pinpoint. I look backward
for the peglegs hobbling
while I walk in cold time. I slither down
a long path mucked to a whirl of dung
and hang onto branches for support.

                    Solitary now
on a balsa bridge across the lily ponds,
I lose all strut.
Skidding along slotted planks, the bridge shakes
as my flimsy tenure shakes. I look out
at sheer rock and sloped dune, stretches
of water lily: something perfect occurred here
long ago, hacked in silence
without men or words — gaunt-winter-perfect
in frame of steel . . .

             I turn back
up the steep track of churned cattle mud
where dead anglers trod, full of their hooked skill,
and riders stumbled, chasing a streak of vermin.
            I scramble up
to slap of sea wind in my face
howling through the lost cemetery.
To the bang of winter, the coming events
and the illusion of action.

John Tripp

DEFENCE OF THE WEST

Castlemartin

The long Panzer huts were deserted,
some windows and a chimney smashed.
Soon thistle, nettle and weed
would win back the ranges.
Farmers stumped again through mud,
tractors jerked forward in lines
like peaceful tanks, and sheep
safely grazed. An occasional bang
was the last of the shots out to sea
to use up the shells. I forgot
why they came to this place.

Their markers and targets
were rusted and sodden by rain,
the crossings greasy from track-oil.
Hooded against the blast off the sea
I heard a gun thump, then a short
gutteral command. Red flags drooped,
Achtung said a tilted board
and overhead
the last chopper went for a joy ride . . .

John Tripp

ST GOVAN

Crossing from Wexford
through that barbarous sea
here you landed first,
preached, built and stayed.
Gobhan — smith, worker of men.

Why? — to bring the Light of Christ
to Lundy's pirates?
To succour the meek farmers of earth and water
they pressed upon?
Because, hounded like an otter,
you found a rock that split and closed
on you like a womb, slipping you free
after their angry going?

Later, stealing the silver bell
that tongued your calling inland
they drew the wrath of angels, lost the plunder
to a mysterious force which laid
its rich voice in rock, giving out song
to the blows of your staff. Was it
for such celestial tricks you held so long
to the cliff's sanctuary, raised a chapel?

Your holy well has dried, cures no blindness,
unbends no twisted bones;
what spirits clung to the place have flown,
though the mud floor is marked by the curious
descending the uncountable steps.

No, what held you is clear:
it was and is the sea.
The sea that bore you crashes
against the brittle cliffs,

breaks and smooths their jaggedness,
works into the bulk of the coast,
below dunes, far below the rasp of cannon-fire
tolling the unholy hour.

Tony Curtis

ST GOVAN'S CHAPEL

Down the seventy-odd
time-scooped steps to it,
the present seemed to drop back.
There was only the sea-lap
and a clear horizon.

Inside the stone kennel
names like Lewis Lewis were cut
two centuries ago. I slithered
in my scuffed suede boots
across the mud of the churned floor
where sailors and thieves
once knelt or hid. Why here?
Why a block of stone
to God on this smash of shore?

I could hear the boom
and whistle of the batteries
above the wave-wash,
    slicing the silence
inside this crude box
that was hacked out of faith.

John Tripp

BARAFUNDLE

The evening was drenched in a pungent seaweed scent
hitting the nostrils, the smell of all decayed time —
salted oceans washing on the one strip,
filling the crevices and seeking out innocent sheep.
At the sand-edge it was so reeking and tough
I thought it might evacuate the farms,
bring down the gulls in flight
and send cattle galloping inland.
The creamed slack of arriving waves
ruffled and fussed at the dark fine sands.

Even in a roseflush summer this shore is
rotted stick and bone and broken shell,
fallen shack and splintered barn
conceding nothing to gloss blue folders
or the town's December dreams of heat.
It is a proud and stubborn line of rock,
impatient under moon channels,
waiting for the late Atlantic lash,
turning a storm-eye on frivollers
but welcoming the rough-weather guest.

John Tripp

A LETTER FROM GWYTHER STREET

This morning, the rain pucker over,
I crossed Barafundle from the sun rocks
To the leaf bank westward. It was fine
And feathery on the uppish wave. My feet
In lifting sand uncovered an older
Sun and a captured wind dry-beached a decade
Ago. But this is October, the salted-down
Summer of the deckspar, colloped by sea-
Worms, and the indestructible layabout
Plastic of the child engineer.

This evening, such brief spirit sinking. I visit
Friends. And first to the grave-spit at Llanion
Where Sian, her W.V.S. uniform in full
Fold, pairs her ankle-bones to the town. Is there
A message for Elis, tied to his cot like
An idiot, his delicate features clouded
Towards a bad-weather eye? Or Doc, cooped up
With his leg off? Or Herbie, lopsidedly
Smiling in the front room, omnivorous,
History and egg slapped on unknowing cheek?

My footprints this morning on Barafundle
Went in and out of the wave, the fine sand
Darkening at the tide-touch and, as I looked back,
Not a mark of my passing anywhere, only
Sea eating the whiter sift, creaming mouthfuls
Of stick and hampered stone and memory
Trapped there. What remains of companionship
Cannot reach them now. Herbie and Doc
And Elis. No eye-light flickers and signals
Identification on their already buried beach.

Roland Mathias

65

STACKPOLE QUAY

A scavenger mole now, grot and sea-wrack
in this cold snow wind where brief family pulp
litters the stirred pebble. The summer's gone over the hill.

Down there at the buffeted, butting slab
swung long rusted grapplers for hooking
bounced smacks to the wall, the phased flotillas of fish.
　　Toppled captains brought slippery
portions of mackerel in. Good grizzled captains salt-whacked,
trawler-buried, all carried down to the sea mist.

John Tripp

THE SPIRIT OF THE PLACE

Find me in the grass.

Find me in the West Wind.

I am between beats of the waves.
Winters I sleep in the seed potatoes
stocked in the dark.

Spring my sap works through tubers
stretching for light. Earth closes on me like a coat.

My engine coughs across the morning-grey farm.

I flower in the straight furrows of the angled steep fields.

I walk the coast path witnessing sun-rise
and fall of globes.

I am the flashing tinsel greed of sky mackerel,
the grey moving of tope deeply beyond Caldey.

I come blackly as cormorant.

With rain I will sweep the litter, rust the cans,
I will take buckets of brine and sluice the piss-smell
from the chapel of St Govan.
I will erase the last scratch of writing,
save that in sand.

My weather eats the oiled guns of Castlemartin.

My surf rides in white, fucks fissures and cave.

I spread my legs in the cliff heather
move with waves.

My cries crack the headland's concrete bunkers,
spike the last war's ghost barrels.

Summers I twist lanes into blindnesses of faith.
I grit through carburettors till they phlegm to a stop;
my nails slough caravans into ditches.

I turn signs.

I rustle the paper bag dropped in the rabbit warren.

Autumn my dusk stirs mice through gaps;
they lodge in the galleries' ledgers,
shred and nest in the gift shops' trash.

I am the last revolution of the screws
of the last tanker nosing into the Haven;
I hang from the Cleddau Bridge,
stare out to the disappearing sea.
I scupper the moth-ball fleet.

My hands dip into rock-pools. Cool.
Anemones flower and close at my touch.

Nights I breathe Calor Gas.

Gulls are my envoys:
they glide and sweep above your heads,
they feed on your droppings.

There! See! And then!

What have you to say?

Tony Curtis

PENINSULA RUN

A shock orange sunball
hit the windscreen
when we crunched off the red beach
at Manorbier, under the ruin.
High-altitude jets
made trails like snail-creep
as we perched on the coast,
two ants mobile in speeding tin.

Flutter of pheasant into hedges,
bits of picnic mess and plastic cup
scattered on the sponge tussock
above the limestone loft of Stack Rocks —
two crags lifting from the sea
breaking on the wine-streaked bulk
of St Govan cliff.
                Then
to Freshwater West, the huge
crater dunes bunkered in gorse
rolling back layer on layer:
skidding through tunnelled driftsand
banked up to the roof,
closing in for a wing-touch
as we curved round to Angle —

that long blockhouse out in the bay
at the end of a western shore
in ramshackle splendour,
at the end of history's province.

John Tripp

from LYDSTEP CAVERNS

Here in these fretted caverns whence the sea
Ebbs only once in all the circling year,
Fresh from the deep I lie, and dreamily
Await the refluent current stealing near.
Not yet the furtive wavelets lip the shore,
Not yet Life's too brief interlude is o'er.

A child might play where late the embattled deep
Hurled serried squadrons on the rock-fanged shore,
Where now the creaming filmy shallows creep
White-horsed battalions dashed with ceaseless roar:
Stirred by no breath, the tiny rock-pools lie
Glassing in calm the blue September sky.

Today the many-hued anemone,
Waving, expands within the rock-pools green,
And swift transparent creatures of the sea
Dart through the feathery sea-fronds, scarcely seen:
Here all today is peaceful, calm and still,
Here where in storm the thundering breakers fill.

Here where the charging ocean squadrons rave
And seethe and shatter on the sounding shore,
And smite this high-arched roof, and wave on wave
Fall baffled backward with despairing roar,
Or fling against the sheer cliffs overhead
And sow these vaults with wreckage and the dead,

Now all is still. Yet ere today is done,
Where now these fairy runnels thread the sand,
Five fathoms deep the swelling tides shall run
Round the blind cave and swallow rock and strand,
And this discovered breast on which I lie
Shall clothe itself again with mystery.

Sir Lewis Morris

IN PRAISE OF TENBY

I beg God's grace, guardian of the parish,
Lord of heaven and earth, profound in wisdom.

A splendid fort stands on the sea's surface:
Mirthful at New Year is a bright headland.
And whenever the ocean booms its boast,
Bards are wont to carouse over mead-cups.

Swiftly the wave surges towards it:
They leave the grey-green sea to the Picts.
And may I, O God, for my prayer's sake,
When I keep my pledge, be at peace with you.

A splendid fort stands on the wide ocean,
A sturdy stronghold, sea-encircled.
Ask, Britain, for whom this is fitting:
Head of ab Erbin's house, may it be yours!
There were throngs and songs in the stockade,
And a cloud-high eagle tracking pale faces:
Before a high lord, before a foe-router,
Far-famed and fierce, they fell into line.

A splendid fort stands on the ninth wave:
Splendid its people taking their pleasure.
Their lively life is not based on disdain,
It is not their way to be hard of heart.
I will tell no lie of my welcome:
Better Dyfed's serf than Deudraeth's yeomen.
Its generous comrades, keeping a feast,
Comprise, in each couple, the best in the land.

A splendid fort stands where a throng provides
Pleasure and praise, and the birds are loud.
Merry its melodies on New Year's Eve
For a bountiful lord, bold and brave.
Before he entered the church of oak,
He gave me wine and mead from a crystal cup.

A splendid fort stands on the sea-coast,
Splendid in granting to each his share.
I know in Tenby, glowing its gulls,
The comrades of Bleiddudd, lord of the court.
Mine was the custom on New Year's Eve
Of a place by a lord bold in battle
And a purple robe and high privilege,
Till I was the tongue of Britain's bards.

A splendid fort stands that is stirred by songs:
What honours I wished for were mine.
(I do not say 'rights'; I must keep my place:
Who learns not this earns no New Year's gift!)
British writings the foremost concern
In that place where waves make their uproar:
Long may it last, that cell where I stayed.

A splendid fort stands, rising high,
Superb its pleasures, its praise far-famed.
Splendid its bounds, stronghold of heroes,
Withstanding the spray, long are its wings.
Harsh sea-birds rush to the rocky peak.
May wrath, banned, make off over the mountains,
And Bleiddudd's be the highest bliss,
His memory kept in mind over mead.
The Lord of harmonious heaven bless them:
May Owain's great-grandson be one with his men.

Anon.

(Translated by Gwyn Jones)

THE ELATE ISLAND

I will show you an island. Come with me
to where, in the west, Wales falls into the sea
and washes her hands of history.

There, like some cretaceous monster at ease
in an ancient ocean — caught in the sea's
quiet trough, come up to breathe and take the breeze —

an elate island lies lazily prone
in the prawn-coloured waters. Backed with bone
of man and mammoth and primeval stone

it stretches luxuriously in the sun
as once it stretched when all the ice had run
to rivers, and again the world was young.

In that moist mist a man stirred and awoke,
crouched in a cave-mouth, kindled fire and broke
the concave blue above him with blue smoke:

its ashes and his own are heaped there still —
a skull that keeps the secret of his skill.
The island basked and burgeoned on until

milleniums mounted to the chosen hour
when, in the rock, another scarlet flower
of flame should bud and petal into power.

Seven saints looked here for heaven and lit a fire
that warmed all Wales. Then monks built up a byre
for beasts and praised God in a Norman choir,

and hid the Glastonbury treasure-trove
in some oblique and satin-sanded cove
or lost green grotto, and the island wove

a weft of weed to waft away all trace,
and drowsed awhile, until the parching pace
of piracy brought Paul Jones to the place

wanting well-water, sweet and grotto-chilled.
A lighthouse put a finger forth to gild
black seas, and monks came back again to build

an alabaster abbey, tall and cool
amid the trees. There in the garden pool
among magenta lilies moorhens drool

their silken legs and goldfish glister through
green lists. And like a water-lily too
the island floats at ease and waits — for you.

Raymond Garlick

CISTERCIANS

Albalanda. Hen Dŷ Gwyn
ar Dâf, Whitland: names wherein
the holy white of that way
is fixed forever. Doomsday
will dazzle with serene light
streaming from the calm snow-white
sierras of all abbeys
of Citeaux. Hives of the bees
of Bernard, within your walls —
whether the sculptured snowfalls
of today, or the ruins
through Europe of all Christ's inns
raised by the white monks — in these
my mind lodges, finds heartsease,
glimpsing through each portico
the lyric rose in the snow.
Samson of Caldey, afloat
on your abbey's silver moat;
Aelred, abbot of Rievaulx:
I seek the secret you know —
the unflawed oneness of song
you lived, heart and word's diphthong:
the lyric, snow fresh, sun warm,
flowering in the nave of form.

Raymond Garlick

BOATMEN

Old Toot they called him,
Though he couldn't hear,
Being deaf and dumb.

At the water's edge he skulled expectantly,
While families queued for the other boats.
Then, sensing rejection, he would wade ashore
And stand at the brink of the beach
Gesticulating,
Pointing towards his empty seats
And the waiting sea.

The other boats had flags in the stern,
Were brightly painted with jaunty names,
And their owners wore peaked caps in the approved
Nautical tradition,
And proudly announced a trip along the coast
To Waterwynch.

Old Toot wore a cloth cap,
And his boat raised no flag.
His idea of a ride
Was straight out beyond the Goscar Rock
To nowhere.

His strange inarticulations
Disturbed the bland holiday mood,
Like an ungainly hermit crab
Slewing across the smooth beach.

His boat invariably put out after the others
Had sailed, with their full complement of passengers;
A few boys unfrightened by his gargoyle face,
Or late arrivers anxious not to deny the children a treat.

We so often denied what he offered,
This old man of the sea.
But I always wished him,
As he floundered among the gulls,
Cargoes more precious than Noah's.

Douglas Phillips

VISIT TO AN ISLAND

1

high on this island's roof I sit, ruling green
fields, rolling dunes spinning beneath my feet

I climbed this hill over gorse lined paths
crushing daisy and bluebell underfoot
to reach the highest point above Priory Bay

from my eyrie, the monastery recedes
fuchsia hedges fade to insignificance
the watch tower shrinks under cliff face
perspective playing age old tricks

figures ascend the quay from the mainland
boat, escaped for an afternoon's curiosity
to this fertile unspoilt island, following

one paved road to the village, they sit
on stone benches writing post cards
sample flower perfumes, pass rock shrines

sprawling in tea gardens cool in shadow
perhaps they glimpse a sandal footed monk
silently trimming golden island gorse

2

I must come down from this hill, my escape is
temporary. cut off here from reality, I extend
myself into landscape, absorbing solitude

but isolation is not for me. my travel bag
lies on grass tufts. I zip it closed, put on
my jacket. now I am ready to go down

another boat approaches the island
nosing cautiously towards landing rafts
oiled keel sliding on green glass

calling me quietly down through giant ferns
to the wrinkled concrete road. I am one
of the shuffling crowd heading towards the quay

the monastery stares out enormous, white walled
fuchsia hedges expand, purple calyxed blooms
burst over my head. I stoop under branching foliage

until turning I see gorse burning the high hill
where one monarch seagull swoops upon crumbs
struts in my place, surveying its kingdom
through pale lidless eyes, ruling for

only a short span, it shakes out wide wings
circles to swoop over boats leaving the jetty
monarch, bird, monk, bursting flower
we are all visitors to this island planet

Alison Bielski

BOATMAN

boatman, in a rain of spray, comes
cockle treading in salt faded shoes
eyes blue mussel shells, white lined
(sight keen as an east wind)
a being more of sea than land

escorted by noisy gull outriders
he patrols his tide-edge kingdom
nodding at boats, bell lobster pots
ropes twisted on driftwood shore
king of the ebb-tide pacing out
his realm through kneeling waves

Alison Bielski

RIPPLE MARKS

In caravans
it needs
a silver twist
or crystal shimmer glint
to track
a life line
on a human hand.

And then
in a laboratory
one polished lens
can silhouette
a structure
more minute.

But at a cliff
in Pembrokeshire
if I were wise
I'd understand
the evidence
of ripple marks,
these petrified designs
of folded lines:
direction flow
of prehistoric tides.

I could then find
more than my fingers hold
and move beyond
the focus of my eye.

Peter Preece

TWO POEMS AT TENBY

1. Epitome

Where the poets thumped the board
about their mead and the chieftain
smiled, the sea is wild.

The rock houses a zoo,
turns its black face to the children
pale from school; the gale
threatens only wintering playboats;
the Tudor Merchant's house has
just shut, it's National Trust.

The church has a light in its chancel;
I clatter down the darkened step;
alone the priest in prayer could be stone.

I find solitude in a bar
high on the walled hill, relive
after half a century's laughter

the shy discovery in gaslight
under five arches of the warmth
of a girl raincoated where mist swirls.

2. Hotel la Normandie

Muzak and crack
of table skittles,
attack and spin
of one-armed bandit,

can I seize
the leather jacket ease
of money with honey
melting at its side?

In from the wild night
it looks good to me, this snug
world of the young
in which I feel foolishly

young. *J'irai revoir*
ce pays lointain of
the arched wall in November
mist, for remember

there's still no end till
the end comes: heart and
belly and throat are good
and I still stand.

Gwyn Williams

RETURN TO TENBY

this early summer holiday morning
before day crowds scatter silence
I walk down the hill below the
slate-roofed harbour church

avoiding broken litter of bottles
ice-cream papers, striped cartons
past rickety boat-houses, over
seaweed steps to the north beach

the tide is out. Glimmering metal
waves dazzle with undulating light
illuminate a man and boy cockling
on the tide-edge, and a sand-yellow
labrador leaping wet shingle

soon the town will throw off its sheets
rising naked to a new day yawning
raising thin arms to summer warmth
cars will nose into parking-places
shop doors creak, open kiosks hang

beach-balls in grape bunches high
above sweet-brimming counters
fishermen in new jerseys and white
cap covers will man wooden stands
propping up chalked lists of trips

and I shall climb Castle Hill to sit
watching the red and blue boats push
out to Caldey Island and flashing
speed-boats tearing tides to rags

I shall observe all from my green eyrie
eagle-eyed, waiting to pounce on new
impressions, ideas, blown fragments
scavenged from this summer holiday morning.

Alison Bielski

TENBY

In winter wound in a cocoon of warm
walls, dug discreetly in, snug as a butler
in a pantry, the essential form

of the place remains but all else sleeps;
even the little waves arch neatly on
the sunlit shore with prim and poodle leaps.

Summer romps in on charabanc and train:
sad men in paper caps consume ice-cream
or candy-floss while sheltering from the rain,

and seagulls rest their red, plebeian feet
upon Prince Albert's alabaster head.
But O the joy of Welsh upon the street.

Raymond Garlick

DYLAN THOMAS AT TENBY

Into the pause, while peppermints were passed
after the strong piano's breathless Brahms,
he walked and took his place, sat down and cast

(expressionless of face) an eye abroad,
moving the carafe with a marked distaste.
His fame proclaimed, he looked politely bored

and crossed his legs and lit a cigarette,
screwing his eyes up at the smart of smoke.
So all was done and said. The scene was set

for speech, and nervously he stirred and spoke —
shuffling the pack of papers on his knee,
at random drew one, stared at it and woke

into awareness. Now the sleeping town
under the wood of Wales sat up and sang,
rose from its river bed and eiderdown

of ducks, strode heron-stilted through the dark
and rode white horses, nightmares from the sea,
across a cantref to this bay's bright arc

and the Noah of a poet calling there
to his creatures to come. Two by two, word
by word they marched from his mouth, pair by pair

to the beat of the drum of his tongue
and the trumpet of his lips. In the ships
of his speech the sage sailed and was sung.

And Tenby, their harbour, attended.
It was October, the month of birthdays.
The saga was nearly ended.

Raymond Garlick

DROUGHT

All rain has been
confiscated,
whined the dry voice
of a summer sky,
presiding with
a classroom master's
petulant control.

And heat
blared back from
patches of scorched land,
forcing that shrinking soil
to crack.

Shimmer had left
the long lake
and streams
reduced by empty weeks
to water-coursing ghosts.

All the dust
of Pembrokeshire
then lifted from a map
of red-brown fields
to powder villages
and white-walled farms alike.

Eventually,
drummed out thunder voices
hidden in the hills,
rain will of course return.

Then you can sit
through the mingle
of dust and water,

see from inside
those smears
slide down across
your window glass.
You will say
to each other
yet again —
All it ever does
in Wales
is rain.

Peter Preece

PEMBROKESHIRE SEAMS

Wales is a process.
Wales is an artefact which the Welsh produce.
The Welsh make and remake Wales
day by day, year by year, generation after generation
if they want to.
— Gwyn A. Williams

1

Between Wiseman's Bridge and Saundersfoot
the coast path runs into coal wagon tunnels
and entrance holes drift down
into the base of a sheer cliff.
A pair of rails points from the path's edge
to launch the memory of themselves out over the bay
in perfect alignment with the next tunnel.

The children run on round: in the dark
there are hollows the shape of a body
they press themselves into. They
burst out at us like predictable ghosts
and we chase them into the light.

On the sand strip below us
the storm has flung a crop
of rotting star-fish.

2

Those years I lived down here,
my parents let the bungalow to English visitors
and we spent the summers in two damp caravans.
We dug the garden patch for potatoes
and the hedge-bank would crumble

with dark shale, flaky stuff on its way
down the centuries to coal.
On a high fire you could coax it
to smoulder and flame.

3

Coal was under us all the time,
the tail of the South Wales seam
surfacing again after the sea.
Shallow, tricky minings worked by families;
the men and children bunched like rats at the levels,
the women at a windlass winching up each
basket of good anthracite with a bent back.
Faults cracked and connived at the work —

this land never saw the rape of the valleys,
though the farmers' sons, worn by the rain
and sick of the smell of the shippen,
walked east and fed the deep pits and the iron.
On day trips their children's children
made their way back, built castles on the beach.

4

My people — the Barrahs, the Thomases
raised cattle and potatoes
on good farming land from Llangwm to Jeffreyston.
Until my great-grandfather
that night in 1908
drunk and late from Narberth market,
roaring down the dark lanes, snapped his pony's leg
and turned the trap over his neck.
Six daughters, and a renegade son away in Canada,
saw the farm sold and split.

We lose ourselves down the years.

Under the earth at Jeffreyston,
wood groans, crack of the bones' cocoon.
A name smoothed away from the slant headstone.

5.

To the north, in the next county,
cottages are put to the torch for the language,
for the idea of community.

A Range Rover coasts to the end of the lane;
shadows, murmurs, a burning bottle
clatters through mock-Georgian panes.
Rebecca rises to purify the tribe.

Not here; below the Landsker
we've been eased out of such extremes.

6.

It is a summer's day. The sea burns
against the eye.
A sky full of laughter and fat gulls.
On the boat to Caldey Island,
looking back you see the fields glint.
The windscreens on the cliff
pearl like standing water.
Deep down lanes a crop of caravans;
sites flower like clumps of nettles.

We trail our hands in the sea.
What did we imagine they would hold?
In the shock of cold they whiten
to the beauty of bones, of coral.

Tony Curtis

OVER SIR JOHN'S HILL

Over Sir John's hill,
The hawk on fire hangs still;
In a hoisted cloud, at drop of dusk, he pulls to his claws
And gallows, up the rays of his eyes the small birds of the bay
And the shrill child's play
Wars
Of the sparrows and such who swansing, dusk, in
wrangling hedges.
And blithely they squawk
To fiery tyburn over the wrestle of elms until
The flashed the noosed hawk
Crashes, and slowly the fishing holy stalking heron
In the river Towy below bows his tilted headstone.

Flash, and the plumes crack,
And a black cap of jack-
Daws Sir John's just hill dons, and again the gulled birds hare
To the hawk on fire, the halter height, over Towy's fins,
In a whack of wind.
There
Where the elegiac fisherbird stabs and paddles
In the pebbly dab-filled
Shallow and sedge, and 'dilly dilly,' calls the loft hawk,
'Come and be killed,'
I open the leaves of the water at a passage
Of psalms and shadows among the pincered sandcrabs prancing

And read, in a shell,
Death clear as a buoy's bell:
All praise of the hawk on fire in hawk-eyed dusk be sung,
When his viperish fuse hangs looped with flames under the brand
Wing, and blest shall
Young
Green chickens of the bay and bushes cluck, 'dilly dilly,
Come let us die.'
We grieve as the blithe birds, never again, leave shingle and elm,

The heron and I,
I young Aesop fabling to the near night by the dingle
Of eels, saint heron hymning in the shell-hung distant

Crystal harbour vale
Where the sea cobbles sail,
And wharves of water where the walls dance and the white
        cranes stilt.
It is the heron and I, under judging Sir John's elmed
Hill, tell-tale the knelled
Guilt
Of the led-astray birds whom God, for their breast of whistles,
Have mercy on,
God in his whirlwind silence save, who marks the sparrows hail,
For their souls' song.
Now the heron grieves in the weeded verge. Through windows
Of dusk and water I see the tilting whispering

Heron, mirrored, go,
As the snapt feathered snow,
Fishing in the tear of the Towy. Only a hoot owl
Hollows, a grassblade blown in cupped hands, in the looted elms
And no green cocks or hens
Shout
Now on Sir John's hill. The heron, ankling the scaly
Lowlands of the waves,
Makes all the music; and I who hear the tune of the slow,
Wear-willow river, grave,
Before the lunge of the night, the notes on this time-shaken
Stone for the sake of the souls of the slain birds sailing.

Dylan Thomas

Biographical Notes

RAYMOND GARLICK: b.1926. An Englishman who has spent a number of years teaching in Pembroke Dock. Founding editor of *Dock Leaves*, his *Collected Poems* is published by Gomer (1987).

JOHN ORMOND: b.1923 in Dunvant, Swansea. Poet and film-maker. His *Selected Poems* is published by Poetry Wales Press (1987).

WALDO WILLIAMS (1904–1971): Poet born into an English-speaking home in Haverfordwest, but is now seen as the most original poet in Welsh this century. Guided by a mixture of Romanticism, Blakean vision and Welsh nationalism, his only book, *Dail Pren* (Gomer), is a classic.

GILLIAN CLARKE: b.1937 in Cardiff, now living near Llandysul in Dyfed. Her *Selected Poems* is published by Carcanet (1985).

SIR LEWIS MORRIS (1833–1907): A native of Carmarthen who devoted much of his life to the fostering of higher education in Wales and to the establishment of a national University.

A.G.PRYS-JONES (1888–1986): Often regarded as the first Anglo-Welsh poet of the twentieth century for whom Wales and the Welsh nation were consistently a source of pride and inspiration.

LESLIE NORRIS: b. 1921. Poet and short story writer who divides his time between Wales, England and the U.S. His *Selected Poems* is published by Poetry Wales Press (1986).

PHIL CARRADICE: Born at Pembroke Dock. A teacher and social worker who writes short stories. His most recent collection is *The Night Time Nasties* (The Meadow Press).

DUNCAN BUSH: b.1946. Prize-winning poet from Cardiff whose latest collection, *The Genre of Silence* (Poetry Wales Press, 1988), is set in the Soviet Union during the Stalin years.

T.E.NICHOLAS (1878–1971): Born at Llanfrynach. A Congregational minister and a founder member of the C.P.G.B., as well as a political journalist and poet. He was twice imprisoned on spurious charges, 'To a Sparrow' being one resulting poem.

JOHN TRIPP (1927–1986): Writer from Bargoed who wrote some of his best poetry during visits to Pembrokeshire. His *Selected Poems* is published by Seren (1989).

JEREMY HOOKER: b.1941 in Hampshire. Poet and critic who lived for many years in Wales. His most recent collection is *Master of the Leaping Figures* (Enitharmon, 1988).

JOHN STUART WILLIAMS: b.1920 in Mountain Ash. Poet and critic. His collection *Dic Penderyn* won an Arts Council prize in 1971.

JEAN EARLE: b.1909 in Bristol, brought up in the Rhondda Valley. Author of three books of poetry, most recently *Visiting Light* (Poetry Wales Press, 1987).

PETER FINCH: b.1947. One of Wales' foremost experimental poets. His *Selected Poems* is published by Poetry Wales Press (1987).

PETER PREECE: b.1936 in Stackpole, Pembrokeshire. Recently, his failing eyesight has diminished his output of poetry.

LEWIS MORRIS (1701–1765): Born on Anglesey. Poet, scholar and cartographer, he is regarded as the prime mover in the classical revival of Welsh learning and writing during the eighteenth century.

BOBI JONES: b.1929 in Cardiff into an English-speaking home. By far the most prolific Welsh-language writer of the latter half of the twentieth century. He is also a critic, short-story writer and scholar.

CLIFF JAMES: Poet and short story writer, born in Pembroke. His latest book is *Cadwgan to Keep a Song* (Imble Publications).

ROLAND MATHIAS: b.1915 at Talybont-on-Usk. Poet, editor, critic and one of the founders of *The Anglo-Welsh Review*. Ex-headmaster of Pembroke Dock Grammar School.

DOUGLAS PHILLIPS: b.1929 in Carmarthen, but teaches now in Derbyshire.

ALISON BIELSKI: b.1925 in Newport. Now lives in Cardiff. Poet and folk lorist, her latest collection is *Eagles* (1983). She has also published several book lets of local history.

GWYN WILLIAMS: b.1904 in Port Talbot. Poet, travel writer and translator. A prolific writer in both Welsh and English, his autobiography *ABC of (D)GW* was published in 1981.

DYLAN THOMAS (1914–1953): One of the most important and challenging of twentieth century poets in English, and perhaps the best known of poets from Wales. A new edition of his *Collected Poems 1934–53* is published by Dent (1989).

The Translators

JOSEPH P. CLANCY: b.1928, American poet and translator. His work includes *The Earliest Welsh Poetry* (1970) and *Twentieth Century Welsh Poetry* (1982), both published by Gomer.

TONY CONRAN: b.1931. Poet, translator and critic. His *Penguin Book of Welsh Verse* was reissued as *Welsh Verse* (Poetry Wales Press) in 1986, and his latest book of poems, *Blodeuwedd* (Poetry Wales Press, 1988) won a Welsh Arts Council Prize.

GWYN JONES: b. 1907. Novelist, story writer, editor, translator. Former Professor of English at UCW Aberystwyth, perhaps best known for his translation of *The Mabinogion*.

The Editor

TONY CURTIS was born in 1946 in Carmarthen, but spent some of his childhood in Tenby. He is author of a number of collections of poetry including *Selected Poems* and, most recently, *The Last Candles* (Seren). A senior lecturer at the Polytechnic of Wales, he has also edited several critical books and written on Dannie Abse and the reading of modern poetry.

Acknowledgements

For Raymond Garlick: 'Dyfed', 'Tenby', 'Dylan Thomas at Tenby' from *Collected Poems*, Gomer, 1987; 'Expedition Skomer', 'The Elate Island' from *A Sense of Europe*, Gomer, 1968; 'Cistercians' from *A Sense of Time*, Gomer, 1972.
For John Ormond: 'Lanscape in Dyfed' from *Selected Poems*, Poetry Wales Press, 1987.
For Waldo Williams: 'Preseli' and 'On Weun Cas' Mael' translated by Joseph P. Clancy from *Twentieth Century Welsh Poems*, Gomer, 1982; 'In Two Fields' translated by Tony Conran from *Welsh Verse*, Poetry Wales Press, 1986. The poems originally appeared in Welsh in *Dail Pren*, Gomer, 1956.
For Gillian Clarke: 'Wild Orchids', 'Seal' and 'Gannet' are all to appear in the forthcoming collection *Letting in the Rumour*, Carcanet, 1989.
For A.G. Prys-Jones: the Estate of A.G. Prys-Jones.
For Leslie Norris: 'At the Sea's Edge in Pembrokeshire' from *Selected Poems*, Poetry Wales Press, 1986.
For Phil Carradice: 'Cromlech Pentre Ifan' appears by permission of the author.
For Duncan Bush: 'Ramsey Island' from *Salt*, Poetry Wales Press, 1985.
For John Tripp: by permission of the Estate of John Tripp. 'Defence of the West: HMS Felicity', 'Defence of the West: Castlemartin', 'At Bosherston Ponds' appear in *Selected Poems*, Seren, 1989. 'Barafundle' and 'Stackpole Quay' appear in *Collected Poems*, Christopher Davies, 1978.
For Jeremy Hooker: 'Sleeping Out on Pen Caer' from *A View from the Source*, Carcanet, 1982.
For John Stuart Williams: the poems are taken from *Green Rain*, Gomer, 1967, and *Banna Strand*, Gomer, 1975.
For Jean Earle: 'Solva Harbour' from *Visiting Light*, Poetry Wales Press, 1987.
For Peter Finch: 'Out at the Edge' is uncollected and appears by kind permission of Peter Finch.
For Tony Curtis: 'Pwllcrochan', 'Jack Watts', 'Land Army Photographs', 'The Weather Vane', 'The Spirit of the Place' and 'Pembrokeshire Seams' from *Selected Poems*, Poetry Wales Press, 1986; 'Travelling' travelling from *Album*, Christopher Davies, 1974; 'St Govan' from *Signals at Sea*, Christopher Davies.
For Peter Preece: all poems uncollected. They appear by kind permission of Peter Preece.
For Bobi Jones: 'Afon Cleddau' translated by Joseph P. Clancy in *Bobi Jones: Selected Poems*, Christopher Davies, 1974.
For Cliff James: 'Landsker' is uncollected and appears by kind permission of Cliff James.
For Roland Mathias: all poems appear in *Burning Brambles: Selected Poems*, Gomer, 1983.
For Douglas Phillips: 'Boatmen' from *Across the Frontier*, Christopher Davies, 1972.
For Alison Bielski: all poems appear in *Across the Burning Sand*, Gomer, 1970.
For Gwyn Williams: 'Two Poems at Tenby' from *Collected Poems*, Gomer, 1987.
For Dylan Thomas: 'Over Sir John's Hill' from *Collected Poems*, permission from J.M. Dent Ltd., and the Estate of Dylan Thomas.

For Joseph P. Clancy: his translation of 'To a Sparrow' by T.E. Nicholas is taken from *Twentieth Century Welsh Poems*, Gomer, 1982.
For Gwyn Jones: his translation of the poem 'In Praise of Tenby' is taken from *The Oxford Book of Welsh Verse*, ed. Gwyn Jones.